JELLYFISH

SUN

T0047570

SIGNAL

FIREFLY

FLASHLIGHT

LIGHTHOUSE

LAMP

SIGNAL

JELLYFISH

FLASHLIGHT

LIGHTHOUSE

PRISM

FIREFLY

SUN

SPARK, SHINE, GLOW!

What a Light Show

WRITTEN BY **Lola M. Schaefer**

ILLUSTRATED BY **James Yang**

Greenwillow Books
An Imprint of HarperCollinsPublishers

For Tavi, the brightest light of all!
—L. M. S.

Dedicated to all the camp counselors
who took us on summer-night hikes to see fireflies.
—J. Y.

Spark, Shine, Glow! What a Light Show
Text copyright © 2023 by Lola M. Schaefer
Illustrations copyright © 2023 by James Yang. All rights reserved. Manufactured in Italy.
For information address HarperCollins Children's Books,
a division of HarperCollins Publishers, 195 Broadway, New York, NY 10007.
www.harpercollinschildrens.com

The illustrations were created digitally in Adobe Photoshop.
The text type is 20-point Gotham Book.

Library of Congress Cataloging-in-Publication Data

Names: Schaefer, Lola M., author. | Yang, James, illustrator.
Title: Spark, shine, glow! : what a light show /
written by Lola M. Schaefer ; illustrated by James Yang.
Description: First edition. |
New York, NY : Greenwillow Books, an imprint of HarperCollins Publishers, [2023] |
Audience: Ages 4-8 | Audience: Grades K-1 |
Summary: "A look at what light is and how
it affects our world"— Provided by publisher.
Identifiers: LCCN 2022020976 | ISBN 9780062457110 (hardcover)
Subjects: LCSH: Light—Juvenile literature.
Classification: LCC QC360 .S33 2023 | DDC 535—dc23/eng20220910
LC record available at https://lccn.loc.gov/2022020976
23 24 25 26 27 RTLO 10 9 8 7 6 5 4 3 2 1
First Edition

GREENWILLOW BOOKS

Light is energy
that helps us see
a path in the dark,

fruit on the tree.

Light shimmers in woodlands
and in the skies.

Light shines in the sea,

Light travels through jellyfish,
air, and glass.
These transparent objects
let light pass.

Light cannot pass
through a rock, tree, or snake.
Their shadows prove
that they are opaque.

Most light is visible
to the human eye,
like neon,

glowworms,

and fireflies.

However . . .
some light is invisible.
Strange, but true!

Like X-rays that show
what's inside of *you*!

Eyes reflect light,
and so do the moon,

metals and mirrors,

a lake at noon.

Light is all colors
wrapped up tight

waiting to show
it's more than white.

Prisms and raindrops
both refract light,
which helps form rainbows—

an optical delight!

With lenses and light,
cells grow in size,

and planets and stars
seem close to our eyes.

Natural light streams
to Earth from the sun,

which plants use to make food
for everyone.

Artificial light
is made by man,

like these bright headlights
on this van.

Some lights warn ships.

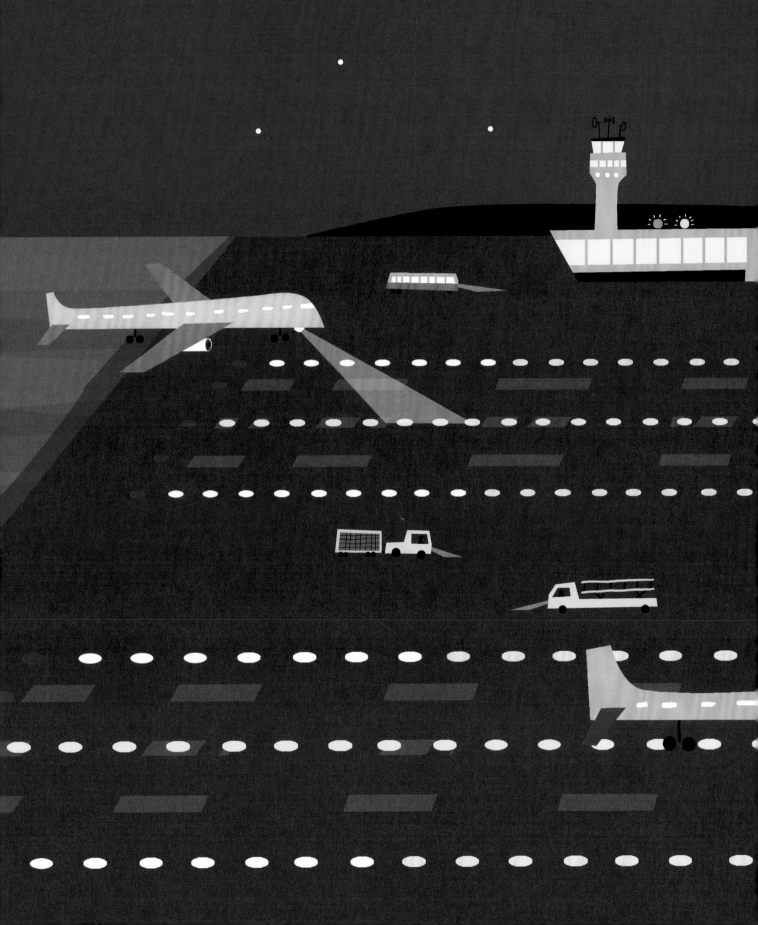

Others guide planes.

And crossing lights signal
oncoming trains.

Light is energy
that helps us see
the world near and far
for you and me.

LIGHT is a form of energy that we can see.

STARS and FIRE are two different sources of NATURAL LIGHT. Our **sun** is a star that emits light that warms Earth and provides energy to growing plants.

ARTIFICIAL LIGHT—such as light bulbs, lasers, candles, fireworks, and glow sticks—is made by man.

Light travels from one place to another in vibrating patterns called WAVES.

REFLECTION takes place when light waves bounce back after hitting a smooth, shiny surface.

REFRACTION happens when light bends as it passes through a clear substance.

WAVELENGTHS of light vary in size. Violet is the shortest wavelength that we can see. Red is the longest.

A RAINBOW forms when sunlight passes through raindrops and bends, or refracts. That light then reflects, or bounces, off the back of the raindrop. As the light leaves the raindrop it bends again, and separates into the colors of red, orange, yellow, green, blue, indigo, and violet.

Look around and find examples of both natural and artificial light that you see every day!